COMFORT & LIES

COMFORT & LIES

poems by
William H. Clamurro

Copyright © 2016 by William H. Clamurro
All rights reserved

Woodley Press
Washburn University
Topeka, Kansas

Cover image and interior photo: Rosalie S. Krenger

Layout and Design: Rosalie S. Krenger

Published in the United States of America
ISBN: 978-0-9908128-4-5
Library of Congress Control Number: 2016945441

First Printing

*To the memory of Gertrude and Phil,
generous readers,
and to
my other readers, past and future*

Contents

Preface
Acknowledgments

Home

At the Oboe Table   5
Home   6
At the Piano   7
Masonry Repair   8
Dead Bird in the Tiffany Lamp   9
Moving the Icebox   10
Wooden Cat   11
Broken Pipe   12
Tuning the Piano   13
Cracked Plaster   14
Cosmicomical Find   15
Cat Science, Part III: The Delusion of Time   16
The Cherry Wood Bowl   17
Exploratory Ants   18
Oboe Lessons   19
Roofing   20
Bat   21
Too Many Books   22
Bat in the Bathroom   23
The Attic Room   24
Closing House   25

Time

Shipwrecks of Time   29
Calculus   30
Insomnia   31
Grace Church   32

Recovered Artefact   33
Birthday   34
Shredding   35
Oral History   36
Old Photographs   37
Note   38
Gouging Cane   39
Letter Recovered   40
Dusting   41
Old Book: *Cien años de soledad*   42
What I Didn't Know at the Time   43
Closing the Account   44
15 March   45
Inner Voices   46
Veteran's Day   47
Diminishing Returns   48
Address Book   49
Maps and Memorials   50
Grandfathered In   51
Passivity   52
Heirloom   53

NATURE

Sycamores   57
Taos, Winter   58
Monarchs   59
Earthquake Oklahoma   60
Shoveling Snow   61
The Sweetgum Tree   62
Cat Science, Part II   63
Magnolia   64
Peonies   65
In the Teeth of Winter   66
Acacia   67
Rosemary Rescued   68
Basil   69
Radiology   70
Pruning   71

April Snow in Kansas   72
Ivy   73
The Dragonflies   74

Travel

Travel   77
War Stories   78
Ghost Town   79
Clearing Station   80
A Note on *La Bohème*   *81*
Sleep Debt   82
El Campo del Príncipe, Granada   83
Packing   84
Cat Science, Part IV: Pulga and Me   85
Photograph   86
Reliquary   87
The River Tormes   88
Frómista   89
Santo Domingo de Silos   90
Alcalá de Henares   91
Poitiers, 11 July 2011   92
Picking up the Pieces   93
Salamanca   94
Puebla   95
Indexing   96

Epilogue

New Student   99
A Coin   100
Body of Stories   101
Sly Artist   102
Renewal   103
Dramatis Personae   104
Cosmos   105

About the Author

Preface

The collection of poems that follows represents a distilling of the poetry that I have written over the course of about ten years. I leave it to each individual reader to decide whatever merit any one of them, or all of them together, may possess. There are a few common themes – some might say that there is a sameness or redundancy to those themes, as well as to the tone and imagery. But again, this is for the reader to decide. These poems, as they were written in a necessarily chronological order, reflect what was going on in my life or certain ideas that struck me at a given moment. But they were transformed into the play of language in ways that were partly deliberate and controlled and yet that, at times, took on a life of their own.

What I need to point out and register with due gratitude is the fact that, over this time and in this process, I have had the good fortune to enjoy the lively interest, support, and wonderfully judicious and creative intervention of some good friends who happen to be superb readers as well. In particular, I would like to acknowledge and thank my two excellent faculty colleagues, Professor Amy Sage Webb and Professor Kevin Rabas of the Emporia State University Department of English, Modern Languages, and Journalism. Both of them have read many of my poems and made very helpful – and sometimes challenging – suggestions. Many of the "fine tunings" of certain poems benefited from their sharp readings. I am also grateful to Kevin for suggesting that I submit this collection to Woodley Memorial Press.

I must also acknowledge, with immense gratitude, the truly inspired readings and contributions of my good friend and former student, Andrew G. Randak (1994 graduate of Denison University, Granville, Ohio). Although by profession he is a banker and financial advisor, Andrew is also a gifted creative writer. He has been, over these many years, a keenly insightful and sensitive reader of my texts. Most of all, as I was culling through over 150 of my poems, I had the inspiration (or perhaps the audacity) to ask Andrew for his advice about which poems to keep and which ones to discard from the collection. He not only helped me "thin the herd," but he also suggested the rearrangement of the poems, taking them out of a mechanically chronological order and grouping them by themes and affinities. This superb stroke started the ball rolling. And with Andrew's sagacious architectural insight, this book came into being.

Someone told me, or I seem to remember, that Pablo Picasso allegedly said that "art is a lie that helps one see the truth." Or words to that effect. If Picasso really didn't say it, he should have. I tend to apply a similar concept to the words or stories that find themselves rendered into poems, or rather, into my poems. My readers often accuse me of ambiguity and evasions – the art of "escape and evasion" as we used to say in my US Army training. This is surely my modus operandi. My ideas and perceptions become fictions ("lies") that might represent a veiled truth for my own recording, or that might open up to another reader a similarity or truth about their own experiences or perceptions. Once a poem has been written it becomes less my personal property than an agent or agency out in the world, with a life of its own.

Acknowledgments

In the interest of acknowledgments I would like to mention again my two ESU colleagues, Professors Rabas and Webb, as well as my former student and excellent reader, Andrew Randak. I am also deeply indebted to Gary Lechliter of the Woodley Memorial Press, who has been my editor for this project. Very special thanks are owed to Ms. Rosalie Krenger, a recent M.A. graduate of the English program at Emporia State, for her superb work in formatting this text for final publication. The poems in this collection have not been published previously with the exception of "Birthday" and "Grace Church" both of which were published in The Flint Hills Review, issue number twenty, 2015, and they are reprinted here with permission from that journal, to whose editors and staff I am most grateful.

COMFORT & LIES

Home

At the Oboe Table

Everything fits into a beige plastic
tackle box, the knives, the slips of cane
to be shaped and tied carefully onto the small
brass cork-rimmed staples where they will
be carved in careful but frustrating work,
over so much time, into the hoped-for reeds.
Spools of bright colored nylon thread and all
the other necessary tools, collected over
so many years. It took all these and a bit
more than half a century for me to learn
about this table, all these implements,
and the uncounted hours, rare success
but so much more failure and futility,
and then to realize that I was here immersed
in acts of unconscious reverence, a kind
of worship or homage. With each new attempt
I reach back in time, in tribute to my teachers
and all the painful modest mystery
of what we shared as we pursued
a sound, impossible magic, and yet
the measure of our years, this dedication
to our mistress of desire.

HOME

The morning sun cascades silent
through the loft high windows,
warms the wide-planked wood floor,
its dark-honey glow a kind of peace;
only the radio intrudes.
The tortoise-shell tabby, an increasingly
perplexing cat, works on her enigmas,
while I gaze dumbly up into the high
comforting space. I've lived here ten years
and a bit more. Has it become my home?
It feels too large, too spaced, both full
and somehow empty, for me and what
remains to me of time. Half lost, I turn away.
The cat stares blankly, unconcerned.

AT THE PIANO

I read once more her beautiful brief note,
my old professor's widow, what she wrote
to tell me he had died, softly, without pain
that spring day on the coast of Maine,
and how he'd asked to be propped up in bed
to see the boats. There was no dread,
just love and family holding near to give
this last farewell. Later I might live
to sit at the piano where I've tucked the card
behind some music, pieces far too hard
for me; I stumble through some bars of Bach,
my vision blurs, as I take stock
of this sweet modest shard of history,
wondering who will write that note for me.

Masonry Repair

One afternoon the mason
comes and we circle the house,
surveying brick and stone, places
where mortar broke off, fallen
away. His binoculars view
too-high chimneys, the skin
of masonry sheathing a home
naked to brutalities of weather
and relentless seasons. I live
too much inside, forget the needs
and complexity of the outer body.
But nudged awake, I now read
surfaces sorely in need of repair.

Dead Bird in the Tiffany Lamp

The shade of the slender floor lamp
is an upturned pyramid of colorful Tiffany
glass. Off in the corner, its light controlled
by a timer, it is not thought about until
the bulb burns out and has to be replaced.
So when the cleaning lady, on her step
ladder, goes up to dust it off, she finds
the sparrow, dead in the glass shade.

Yet another intrusive mystery. How did
the bird get in? A misguided flight down
the chimney? I never saw it, alive or dead,
nor did the Cat play any part; I asked her.
Once more I must surrender to a strange
and sinister conundrum, a house that grows
too large, fissured, while still a shelter in space
and time, now a story I no longer understand.

Moving the Icebox

After fifteen years in its not-quite-silent
place, the refrigerator has to be moved out,
slow and careful, on wheels all but never used.
Removal from its spot unavoidably reveals
the dust that has sifted in, as if a secret gathering.
Also exposed are objects tossed and lost,
cat toys scooted underneath by a playful paw
that later tries but cannot reach; so many
small balls of crumpled paper, batted across
the floor until they zip into the dark recess.
Invisible, but only for a time. The tomcat
of the paper balls fell ill and had to be
put down. This happened years ago.
The refrigerator move becomes a winding
back, almost retrieval of lost years.

Wooden Cat

The spindly ficus that I thought
(or hoped?) would die has come back
with a vengeance. Despite neglect it gives
profuse proliferation of new leaves.

A subtle shower of sticky goo drifts down
onto the bare oak floor, onto the carved
green figure of the wooden cat that sits
on a high thin table, a kind of pedestal.

This cat was long ago a gift from a friend
who later found it necessary to break
off bitterly with me. So now it sits,
each passing year meaning less

yet somehow more, to gather dust
and the mist of sticky gum invisibly
dropping down from the silent tree.

Broken Pipe

For so many decades invisible, tucked
between walls of plaster and tile,
piping water to a bathroom sink,

until corroded and fatigued, the metal
breaks and unperceived the flow
invades and floods the floor below;

a catastrophe only discovered later,
a basement that half a century had filled,
wall to wall, with objects, boxes, furniture,

priceless and worthless, beyond account.
Later you try to salvage what you can,
and while some things survive, in fact

this accident has changed your inner
world of hope, fear, desire, for you
had become one with your mementos,

and this ruptured pipe was just the soft
yet ruthless touch of time on your shoulder
telling it will soon be time to move.

Tuning the Piano

The Cat and I sit silent, half distracted
on the couch, listen to the piano tuner,
his patient painful plinking on the keys,
one note at a time, trying to rectify
too many years of dormancy, neglect,
to fix the action of the keys, bring
something back. This small upright sat
for many years in my mother's house
in New Mexico, another temporary place,
until she knew to slowly close things down
and had this old piano shipped to me
in Kansas. She said "Maybe you'll want
to play it, now and then." It was
another ending stage. So at times
my clumsy hands plunk through
a simple piece on her piano, sitting
in this sun-filled room. The process done,
the tuner packs away his tools, I pay
his bill, he leaves, and for a moment
there's silence as the piano waits
for the return of my uncertain touch.

CRACKED PLASTER

Lying supine in bed, just now awake,
I look at the ceiling and see the crack,
and then I notice that a similar
connected line of rupture traces
down the wall, marks a painful shift,
the ground itself beneath this house
of more than eighty years, stone
and brick, concrete base rooted
in this soil, speaking of its age.
The earth itself, wounded and cursed
by long and brutal drought, gives up
its comforting illusion of solidity,
and like the mortals seeking home
and shelter here, heaves a silent sigh
of its captivity to time and change.

Cosmicomical Find

We always suspected it was so, but
the Oxford American Desk Dictionary locates
the entry for "oboe" between their definitions
for "obnoxious" and "obscene." Slipped in
with oboe, of course, we find oboist to share the curse,
the oboe as instrument of torment and indiscretion,
erotically too crude except to slyly mention.
And this is where and how I've found myself engaged
in petty crimes of music, perpetrating pain not just
upon myself but also on the innocent audience.
Thus it makes sense to find obnoxious oboe obscenity
further framed by well-earned "obloquy"
and a final deflation of "obscurantism"
where, at its most innocuous, it ends.

Cat Science, Part III: The Delusion of Time

They know a different shape of time.
Alas, we wretched humans are duly cursed
by learning how to count. Quantities
and objects placed in some ordered line.

And because our necessary memory
was contaminated with imagination,
visions reconfiguring the past
while likewise scanning a blurred horizon

that someone named the future,
we set ourselves along the arcs
and trajectories of time, as if
to understand and justify our lives.

Cats know the pathos and futility
of our entrapment in this mirage.
For them there is no line of time
but just the warm uncounted circles

of each day, sun and night, their servants
feeding them dutifully, then quiet, off
to find a proper place to sleep
back into their soft and spiraled dreams.

The Cherry Wood Bowl

Graceful, yet so small and light,
barely larger than my two hands
cupped, to hold its warmth,
almost the tone of sun-tinged bodies,
textures that will contrast against
the pallor of a young man's flesh.
The lip curves outward, wide
opening to you on a day in March,
to be filled with random coins,
peanuts, or nothing at all
other than its open upward gesture
of holding, silent, not empty
but filled perhaps with memory
and the mute perplexities of
a certain distanced love.

Exploratory Ants

Not a true invasion like the periodic infestations
of my mailbox that stands defenseless by the curb,
these random ants, just two or three at a time,
wander about on the smooth white porcelain
of the sink and tiles of the upstairs bathroom.
They seem to be searching. But for what?
Or are they simply lost? Ant-miles far away
from their teeming ant-hill home. Annoyed,
I throw them into the bowl, a small-scale
Burial at Sea; and I ponder such intrusions:
spring arrives, and so our plants and insects
open and resume their cyclic moves in time.
The earth, too huge yet too mysteriously small.
Arrivals of exploratory ants. Perhaps myself,
also in search, insignificant and lost
on this globe increasingly too vast.

Oboe Lessons

I've learned . . .

that every time I raise the instrument
to lips and lungs, to coax a stream of sound,
it is a struggle never cleanly won;

that all my patient carving of each reed
is a blind search for perfection,
beauty intimate yet out of reach;

that this slender hollow cone of silver keys
and warm dark wood obsesses me
for years as it leads and mocks me through
heartache and bliss, the labyrinths of music;

that I grow old, my play enriched in depth
and subtlety, while body's strength declines.

And yet I cannot stop or finally lay aside
this source of love and loss.

Roofing

Autumn settling in, the indicated time,
old roof shingles break off, slowly yielding
in the fight with weather and the years.

Roofers climb carefully over steep pitches,
dormers, the creases where one plane meets another;
skillfully peeling off slates worn by so many seasons,

study the planks, find stretches of rot to be replaced.
Inside I listen to their efforts, thinking how
their pounding measures out another time as well.

The work will end, a house renewed yet older too,
while memory slowly closes round us like returning
winter wet and darkness, waiting in and for another age.

BAT

Startled by a sudden fluttering of black,
abruptly flying through the open door
into my unsuspecting office, I try
to evade, fall from my chair,
stumble hard onto the floor. Was it a bat?
And then, although it's here, there is
no trace. Hidden perhaps behind
decades of shelved books, there by
years of sentiment, neglect.

The shocking black invader came
to tell me that this place has never
been immune or safe. And then
another message comes, telling me
that an old friend, still recovering
from surgery, has had a minor stroke.
Invasive ravages, random, then they
disappear without a trace.

Too Many Books

The small coffee table, warm wood
of walnut and cherry, overflows
with stacks of books and magazines
that this life won't give me sufficient
time to read. Through the tall windows
this day's light filters low and gray,
as if in wait. Nearby in a corner
of the couch, curled on the gray-brown
Mexican blanket, the tortoise-shell tabby
appears to sleep, as on all mornings.
But one suspects that she mainly dreams
of feline pleasures, food, and the fine
absurdity of this foolish old man,
writing some new lines, that
and his baffling piles of paper.

Bat in the Bathroom

Suddenly it is just there
as I glance into the room,
a dark form hanging on the white
diaphanous curtain, eerie
and motionless against the light.
Startled, fearful perhaps, I close
the door, think what I should do.
Later I trap it in a plastic bag,
carefully take it out, drop it
into the winter cold, gone only
for a while perhaps,
a message that I do not want to read,
intrusion or reminder that this space
never was safely or completely mine.

The Attic Room

Here yet not quite here, a dream as much
or more than a warm enclosing space,

held gently, tucked beneath the high-pitched
rafters arching like the skeletal ribbed hull

of an inverted ship. Both light and darkness
filter through a small window, eye gazing east.

I want to read a well-loved text
here in the dark and forbearing embrace

of winter, books gently housed high up,
safely wrapped in the wings

of memory, recurrent hope. And you?
Another book, deep part of the dream.

Closing House

I move through this dim familiar house
      as if in dream,
old pictures line the walls of a narrow
      dusty hall, and while
the world outside might be washed
      in vibrant sun,
this interior is now eternally shrouded
      in a dusk of mind
and memory, and all about, this chaotic
      catalogue of time,
substantial in the clutter of old furniture,
      unread books, and objects
piled one upon another. I contemplate
      the desiccated flowers,
pick up a piece of ancient crochet,
      silent witnesses,
parts of a twilight realm that we
      will soon relinquish
and close down.

Time

Shipwrecks of Time

Barely aware, I give all over to the rule
of time. Both flesh and memory grow slack.
I try to read each object yet hold back
against the accidents of loss. The days a spool

of recollections and mementos kept
part of a story I endlessly retell.
I shuffle though old letters, some too well
preserved, so many photographs, except

the ones I really want to find and hold,
as if one more reading of a face, a time
would let me put it all in place, away

yet always here, the hope that won't grow old,
while beyond these walls the garden riots,
I gather up possessions toward that final day.

Calculus

In his high school yearbook note
he said he hoped to be a teacher
of French someday. Instead he taught
mathematics, brilliantly, for many years,
and luckily for me, he was my father.
So I got through high school math
decently. I thought that I'd be good
at math. I asked him, but he said no,
said that I didn't have the flair.

Now half a century gone, my father
dead for twenty years, I wonder back
into those too-elegant ideas,
conic sections: circles and parabolas,
hyperbolas, the concept of limits.
How, struggling through calculus,
I never understood the simplest idea.
But now their mysteries, the magic signs
enthrall me, the concept of the asymptote,
bending toward a line, infinities, as I go
asymptotically toward our point of end.

INSOMNIA

Awake, but only half, and halfway through
a night when I'm sorely in need of sleep,
uncomfortable in the sweat and tangle
of a bed just past midnight and alone,

I don't want to get up, adjust the small
oscillating fan on the dresser aimed
a bit too high. Almost exhausted from
my struggle to dig back into unconsciousness,

I wait, from one fit to the next, and when
I do slip once again through half-sleep into
another dream, I'm dreaming vividly
that I have insomnia, but the woman

nearby says, "no, it's just a symptom of
the dread disease from which you soon will die."
And now I can't be sure about what side
of wake-sleep's border I'm left stranded on.

GRACE CHURCH

A squat dark sandstone church, uphill
from the house where I grew up, a place
and time that slip into vague past. Inside
the dim old murals, almost pre-Raphaelite,
on the vaulted ceiling. Soft winter light
sifts through the stained glass windows. I had
forgotten their careful, complex workmanship.
The priest arrives, a woman, older
than I thought she'd be. We all go out
into the January cold, and by the wall
of aging plaques, each name with its pair
of dates, there in the ground the small hole
has been dug, space enough for mother's ashes.
Prayers are said. We each take turns, gently
dropping earth upon the ash, to share
this laying down, this moment of return.

January 16, 2015

Recovered Artefact

Things hidden have a way of coming back.
Thus when I rummage about in a small
cardboard box, a smaller box within, where
I keep sewing tools, needles and thread,

I come upon a square thin metal box
that I must have forgotten, or tucked away
yet kept for reasons perhaps once known
but that now seem long lost. There inside

a folded-up and faded piece of paper,
an Army notice dated 12 June 1970,
my name slightly misspelled, the heavy
tarnished silver Combat Medical Badge,

from a time, my assignment in Vietnam,
a fragment of that young damaged man
I was, lost and yet now rediscovered
in a battered metal box.

Birthday

My older brother gently wheels our aunt
into the sun-washed room, an afternoon,
late August, to her birthday party, soon
into her second century. I can't
fully believe the wonder of it all.
She frowns at first, lost in the mists of age,
confused, but then the birthday cake awakes
a pleasured smile, past memory, enthralled
by simple joys of sugared icing. She picks
carefully, eating at her own slow pace.
I sense it as a secret miracle, this place
in time. Rose is here and yet is slipping on,
and in the question of her startled look,
she tugs me with a gentle thread along.

Shredding

Somehow I felt the moment had arrived
to rifle through these silent files, absurd
accumulated years, manila folders
holding mind-numbing scores of pages,

papers, names and calculated grades
of countless students, some well-remembered,
others I simply can't recall. I take
these confidential records to the shredder,

and patiently, three or four sheets
at a time, I feed them to a machine
that renders them ribbons of oblivion.
Here and there I spy a certain name tied

to a year, and I cannot escape the sense
that these shreds make up the fabric
of a slowly slipping memory, a career,
threads of time lost in this dusty sphere.

Oral History

The dental hygienist pokes in
and patiently scrapes away the build-up
since my last visit here. Not just
an accounting of the teeth, parade review
of the grimly aging squad, but a reading
of the bleak betrayals of the mouth,
odd discolorations behind the teeth,
the gums, dark stains on the roof,
anomalies that intrigue but she can't explain,
my wretched and revealing cave, hapless book
a portal of unwise ingestions, futilities of talk.
I lie there supine and defenseless, pored over.
When I leave, the mouth feels weirdly clean,
fragmentary secrets bared but still the mystery.

Old Photographs

The battered cardboard box sits unopened, silent
ten long years, tucked in a corner of a room
I enter every night, fearful of its nagging call.

Finally it must be moved, the contents sifted,
sorted out, the scores of letters bundled
without order, kept I don't know why,

and worse, the photographs, hundreds;
black and white, and some in color, leached
out and blurring, edges curling, warped with age,

too long sequestered in the moldy twilight
of forgetting and neglect.
So sitting on the floor of the bright high-

ceilinged room, I shuffle through them all,
pushing myself to throw the dross away,
but stopping, pained and undecided

at the pictures of family and old friends,
some I barely recognize at first, and most
perplexing, these versions of my former self.

Note

Increasingly my dreams are sinister,
begin in unfamiliar cities, a house,
and soon a person I might know
has disappeared, abandoned me,
the place grows dark, confusing.
I cannot find my car. I search
for something like a bathroom,
a shelter, the familiar face
that was there just a while ago.
Eerie displacements, thefts,
subtractions of desire.
I wander in a parallel universe
where natives speak a language
half-broken and misunderstood
except for one last crazy lad,
with gleaming tiger eyes, a sly
golden smile, sharing only half
his eerie musical and mythic tale.

Gouging Cane

A simple yet demanding task that I
do patiently when my supply runs low.
The slender cylinders are soaked, and then
the work begins. The three-bladed flèche

splits each tube, I run each piece through
the filière, then chop it to the proper length
to fit into the gouger that scoops out
the pith, down to improbable thinness.

It requires such close attention, time,
and careful as I am, I often wound the tip
of my left index finger, a small smudge
of blood left on the cane. My teacher,

who died seven years ago, taught me how
to go through this process. He truly was
an oboist, a genius. I will never distantly
approach his skill or art, as each year

robs me of stamina and strength.
So little remains. But I go on, pursue
this gentle struggle with the wood,
an act of devotion, quiet gratitude.

LETTER RECOVERED

It's one of my peculiar tics, I tend
to slip old letters, pictures, notes, a card
between the pages of a book, one
among dozens cluttering the shelves

that time and anxiety have made
the dark chaotic library of my life.
So then it comes as no surprise
to find a letter tucked inside the cover

of my bilingual copy of the Holy Quran,
and it is dated from two thousand five,
sent by the oboe teacher from my youth,
written in the year before his death.

The handwriting is so legible that I know
he must have dictated it to his wife. By then
his sight and ability to write were unequal
to the task. The letter told me about pieces

for oboe that I might consider finding, try
to learn, perhaps perform. A recovered letter
tumbling from a curious book long laid aside
reminds me of a gratitude left incomplete,

a message I failed to send and yet
a fragile bridge back to a privileged time,
unworthy of the music he'd given me,
but striving to be loyal to his legacy.

Dusting

As young kids our mother had us dust
the furniture in our house in New Jersey,
flat surfaces if we could reach them
and the ornate heavy legs and horizontal
supports of the dining room table.
I'd crawl on hands and knees, dusting,
exploring the furniture from below.

Decades later that old house, glimpsed
briefly on a passing visit, seems small.
I now live far away, in a house I chose
because it looked comprehensible in size.
But slowly it has grown too large,
and for reasons I can't explain,
more dust accumulates, its sources
are places that I fear to contemplate.

OLD BOOK: *CIEN AÑOS DE SOLEDAD*

I cannot bring myself to discard or suppress
this book, thin paper cover reinforced
with cardboard, the spine taped over
and over again. Someone bought it for me
at Schoenhof's in Cambridge, Mass.,
and it was new in nineteen sixty-nine —
on the last page one reads the lines
"Se terminó de imprimir en offset,
el día 28 de mayo del año 1969
en los talleres gráficos de la Compañía
Impresora Argentina, S.A., calle Alsina 2049,
Buenos Aires." Later in that same year
it flew with me, a young fearful Army medic,
to the jungles of Vietnam, where its pages
would absorb the mold and tensions
of that time and place, surviving magically intact,
and I, almost as fortunate, would bring it back,
my companion giving comfort and escape,
and now a link of memory that must be kept.

What I Didn't Know at the Time

Network of brooks and ponds, veined
through slender shaded parks, bottomed
among the gentle hills rising in sequence
westward from the coast, ribs of earth
cradling a density of towns, continuous
infinity of homes and the place where I
played out the follies, never resolved
confusions of a childhood that would
decades later leave me lost, far away,
in an emptiness of west, cut off forever
from the softly beautiful, perverse illusions
of New Jersey landscapes, the ghost
of an idea of home, now living out
the breakage of one bond after another,
conundrums of failed companionship,
into the bitter depletions of solitary age.
And yet a vision of a dark-skinned child
crouching by the brook to watch
the water skeeters dancing magical
on the pulsing and transparent skin.

Closing the Account

Although she died almost a month ago,
I only now have time to make the drive
up to a bank branch in Topeka. I've
brought the statement, documents to show

that I'm the second name on the account.
I sign some forms. The woman cuts a check.
It's all in order. Leaving, I reflect
on how this insignificant amount

means so much less than closing down
a near forgotten, cherished link
to my mother in her slow decline. I think
how less and less it matters what we own.

The drive back home has left me empty, numb,
an intimation of what's yet to come.

15 March

A day of no distinction, really, just
a date that comes each year
with or without memory or obligation.
The house was cleaned the day before,
so that when I returned I found
the daffodils she'd picked and left behind
in two small vases, improvised,
and windows opened to let spring air
course through the rooms. I thought
how magical these transformations are.
I twist a small brass kaleidoscope,
lost in pointless change of lovely shapes,
trying to conjure back a long lost student,
now grown old and resolutely alien to me,
while here spring's premature arrival
proffers a hint of new and bitter breakages.
Time's losses and accumulations mount.

Inner Voices

Betrayals of the sense of hearing,
not really in the ear, but deeper down,
flawed nerves connecting to the brain,
my tinnitus is a constant high
metallic buzz, a tormenting,
disembodied worm of sound.
Maybe other frequencies
also break down, slight deafness
slowly coming on, poetic justice,
a punishment deserved because,
as now I see, I've always loved
music far too much. Yet still
as I listen to familiar symphonies,
Mozart, Brahms, I hear so much
more clearly the inner voices,
not just soaring treble melodies
and inescapable foundations
of the gently throbbing bass,
but the soft supporting frame,
the interwoven threads,
perhaps a prelude to voices
I may hear when this
and all my other music ends.

VETERANS' DAY

The eleventh of November
returns each year on the step
of winter. As years mount up
my own brief soldier life fades
back in time and space. Yet
I remain a veteran, my past
keeps circling back in memory
real as the jungle tedium,
violence and heat. A veteran
is one who has survived,
remainder and reminder
of those I knew
but never would return,
except as names incised
on a black stone wall,
a gash into the silent earth
against the quiet park,
linking us to others,
a shared and brutal past.

Diminishing Returns

My Mom's Dad was a modest, skillful engineer,
pressed by hard times, the Depression, moving
from one city to another, Paterson, New Jersey,
to Buffalo, then back again.

I am a child, too young to understand,
as he tells me how he explained
to the visiting Russian engineers,
the phenomenon of diminishing returns,

how doubling the diameter of the mirror
first also doubled the length of the beam.
But at a certain point further increases
did not yield the same result, how we reach

thresholds of limitation. Not long after,
he would die, in the smallest bedroom
upstairs in our house, but at least not alone.

Only much later would I recall these lessons,
how diminishing returns embrace other laws,
beyond mysteries of light stabbing skyward
through the night.

Address Book

A small six-ring black vinyl book,
five and a half by four inches, pages
some new added, others weeded out,
names and addresses pasted in on tiny
labels, some written over, old pages
tattered, worn; new leaves added only
when space is made by taking others out.
Periodically I flip through the whole
chaotic listing, barely alphabetical, note
the names of people now deceased,
and others merely distanced by the turns
of time, geography, the changing arcs
of separating lives. Sometimes I draw
a gentle pencil line through the name
of one now dead. I hesitate to take
such pages out — where would they go?
— paused in the inertia of love.

MAPS AND MEMORIALS
for Eduardo Jaramillo (1957-2008)

The cruel and cold deceptions of maps,
the trickery of schematic space rendered
on the easy reassuring flatness of paper,
a plan that slyly pretends to tell you
where you are, while with a practiced
con-man's nonchalance it fails to mention
true distances, or leg and lung-straining hills,
confusions of topography, landmarks, buildings
out of place. As here in Charlottesville, Virginia,
whose stately university — all warm red brick
and graceful white columns, neoclassical tranquility —
you thought would be intimate and welcoming,
an easy and comprehensible space, only to find it
somehow too wide, harsh, frenetic in a way,
as you hike up one too many hills, dismayed
at the toll of your own old age, or at
the sad memorial and why you've come.

Grandfathered In

So finally we both fell victim to
the lurking hazards of our mundane roles,
a rare convergence of two travelers, poles
apart in years yet somehow linked in true

devotion, curiosity not waning
despite my weariness and slowing age,
interests rekindled by your joyous rage
to read, write, and devour, as you are gaining

both knowledge and your full identity,
while I look on in wonder at this late
and happy accident of work and fate,
a triumph that I've had the luck to see.

The real-life father generates the son,
but by your spell, a grandfather is won.

Passivity

No letter can manipulate reply.
The perverse thrill to read a pleading note,
abject desire, a tightening of the throat.
You sense it, like a dim pathetic cry

for just a gesture, giving back a word,
some evidence the linkage still exists.
But now your closed life quietly resists
all interest in voices long unheard.

It's so much easier: the elegance
of total silence, musing as you gaze,
eyes blue as sky-reflecting lakes, the chance

to scroll back through neglected years, to days
and words before that shattering offense;
a chill that neither time nor guilt allays.

Heirloom

Fragile quiet miracle, survival now through
a hundred years, barely touched by the dust
of forgetting, loss, this intricate gem, a mandolin,
the curve of its body impossibly intact,
pear-shaped tortoise shell, incised a map
of Italy, and round the upper edge
minute escutcheons, heraldry of cities,
provinces; inset photographs of royalty,
leaders of the unification; designs
and figures in mother of pearl.
Somehow it endured, in silence
waiting, its metal strings still capable
of music. More valuable than renewal
of old sound perhaps the link back
to and through so many years, parts
of a family now so dispersed, faded like
inset photographs, still trying to recall.

Nature

Sycamores

Trees? Not quite authentic trees. More
a sort of monstrous extenuated weed,
they masquerade as brethren of the maples,
oaks, less civil than the grim but consoling
evergreens. Persistent local vandals,
my sycamores recurrently throw down
their brittle, gnarled and ugly branches
to clutter and outrage the lawn.
And with autumn they spill their huge
obnoxious leaves, God's junk mail,
and I am tasked, repeatedly, to police
the grounds. I look up, not knowing
whether I should curse or mumble
wry humiliated thanks to these evil trees,
sentinels, relentless markers of my place
within the cyclic lines of time and space.

Taos, Winter

The grasp of cold is sharp and different here,
a stab not in the flesh but an extreme
of soul, a certain dryness, how I seem
defenseless to this thinner sheath of air.

So once more in this season I return.
Winter begins, a calendar count ends.
Each added year is loss; what one intends
has not been reached, and this is all we learn.

I'd want the peace of mountains to be more
than cyclic witness to my solitude,
desire and body yielding to the crude

demands of time, yet knowing that before
this trip you simply were not here to share
the touch that makes cold possible to bear.

Monarchs

On an absurdly clear blue noon
I sit at lunch, glance out through
tree tops, north into the perfect sky
past upper branches, foliage, to look
at nothing, nothing but the calming
emptiness of air, when briefly fluttering
first one, a glimpse of gold, bright
orange with that tracery of black,
and then another, and more, circling
in their magic random dance,
the Monarchs, stopping here,
their moment of late summer flight
from north to south, valleys in Mexico;
but for a midday in September Kansas,
points of color, across my fading vision,
echo of souls in transition from life
on earth to a blue beyond perhaps,
or merely joyous flags of season's end.

Earthquake Oklahoma

In a darkness of October night, the vast
tranquility of our prairie, even far away,
here, it is dimly felt, barely a twitch, as if
a question, except that the cat resting
on the couch beside me takes note.
The earth has shrugged, and somewhere
this shift and creaking of its secret plates
will have left damages, a crack in plaster,
the stonework of a wall. And the idea
of our familiar solid earth is rattled,
though we have always known
that deep beneath all we can see
or touch the real enclosing body lies
perhaps only asleep but always in wait,
while we race about as if our surfaces
could always be the safe home
of our futile and delusive dreams

Shoveling Snow

As if an irony of climate response
to the too long punishments of drought,
a snow fall, voluminous, stops up a day,
carves out a stretch of time, a pause.
Inadequate as body and spirit may be,
I nonetheless go out to shovel off a path,
free up the driveway as much as possible.
That I can even do this heavy task
despite lost strength, toll of another year,
is subtle reassurance, a modest victory.
I rest now and then, lean on the handle
of a blue plastic snow shovel, flimsy as
my own unaccustomed body, and smile
at a still gray sky, the cold, a small path
cleared through one more winter's storm.

The Sweetgum Tree

The sweetgum tree in my front yard vies
with sycamores for the vandalism prize,

relentless scattering its brown spiny pods,
brittle sea urchins underfoot, mischief from the gods,

a mess and yearly message that reminds
me of the indifference of nature as it unwinds

its processes and rules of growth and slow decay.
I make half-hearted efforts to rake, but they

are infinite and crafty, blanketing the ground,
tucked in the grass, tree roots, never all found.

The last ones, elusive, overlooked, later reemerge,
to mock me like bad memories, a guilty urge.

Vexed, I surrender, remove a tattered garden glove,
while harsh stars sting like lost and fractured love.

Cat Science, Part II

The cat and I are doomed to mis-communicate.
Or is it that I constantly impute
mind and sensibility to this mute
tortoise-shell tabby? Her patient wait

for me to sense or figure out her need,
what tedious attentions she requires,
distance or contact, cool to all desires,
or simply something new on which to feed.

I wonder if she'll ever learn to read
the dark book of my numbing solitude;
but we're each other's riddle. Futile, rude,
to demand science when we can only plead.

Magnolia

Blossoms awkward and extravagantly large,
white, mauve tinged, always come too soon,
imprudently ahead of the true arrival
of spring's needed warmth. As if the gnarled
old tree, rough embittered limbs, indifferent
or impatient, would not wait. A late snow
might blast their mute returning pages,
but this undaunted plant stands immune
to any sense or brush of human time.
I read the battered branches, soon
withered petals, and cannot but recall
a frail and aged woman fading beneath
a very different law of seasons,
beyond all images, one last photograph.

Peonies

Resolute, sudden but silent, with the turn
into spring, the thick green leaves explode,
spread their bushy base, dark and strong,
piercing forth from their profusion, on thin
insistent stems. Small tight boles reach
into empty air, miniature hard fists
raised to the sky, but still closed,
waiting for the teams of patient ants
to nibble at the yearning seams.
They'll come and eat, liberate the huge
outrageous blooms, symbiosis of need
and desire. The flowers will not last long
beyond the bludgeoning of wind and rain.
Merely a moment, a soon discarded stage
of spring. I marvel at their mindless
gentle indifference. The calm tenacity
of flowers marks the return of a season
but also steals another year, part miracle,
part wound. We appreciate color and life
if we willfully forget the reckoning
of human years, the fact that we
won't endlessly return with them.

In the Teeth of Winter

Snow day. Our weary schedules put on hold.
Flakes sift down sparsely, less than a blizzard
of the mind, and I think, the relativity of cold.
Beyond tall windows a pine tree shudders
in wind that sweeps the snow off sidewalks
to pile it elsewhere, drifts forming against
a sheltering wall. Mystic hourglass of snowfall,
winter is about hiatus and the need to give
a certain stretch of time to thought.
Gesturing against the grip of numbing cold,
I slide my hand across your naked warmth,
but only in the dreamscape of a winter
of memory and desire, and if I think of spring,
it's with the knowledge that once again
you will not be there.

ACACIA

I come to realize I've totally lost count
of how many years you've lived there,
on that quiet road named Acacia.
I dimly recall the narrow lane, a small
half-secluded house, but do not know
the tree itself. I find some photographs,
information on this sturdy, spiny tree,
bright yellow flowers, thorns sinister
as medieval weaponry. Your own
unyielding rectitude stretches
a silence out to uncertain age,
the drift where any memory
of our times together dissolves,
beauty into myth, and you
still in my guilty conscience,
a persistent thorn.

Rosemary Rescued

The brutal drought of summer
that killed so many other plants
somehow spared most of the herbs,
the slender strip of garden huddled
at the red brick wall,
but the rosemary was overshadowed
and stunted by profusions
of an unruly tarragon.
When the chill of autumn shriveled
all the others, the rosemary was left
intact but spindly. Fearing winter
possibilities, I dug it out,
put it in a pot,
and brought it into the house,
persistent yet frail, pungent
from summer's bitterness,
to keep company with mine.

BASIL

As the days were turning colder
I thought to bring the surviving
basil plant inside, already withering
in its too-big terracotta pot,
an accidental plant, from seeds
thrown in I don't remember when.
Though sheltered, it will not thrive
much longer, its flourish point is past.
What green remains has lost its gleam,
grows gray. The spindly stems
gradually turn black. The gift
of its sweet sharp smell fades
into winter interior, this increasingly
closed and silent house, December.

Radiology

In the dim half-light of the x-ray room
I stand patient, curious, stripped to the waist,
as the young technician does her job,
indifferent to the slack hirsute trunk

of one more ageing, nameless man.
I'm here to give myself so she can take
pictures of a skeletal interior, what is
unseen but always there, articulations.

Later, the specialist and I will look
at images, read secrets of my inner book,
discuss some options to relieve the pain,
well knowing that there's no sure remedy.

This inner ache is time itself; a ghostly hand
on the shoulder of what remains, a destiny.

Pruning

In any necessary season it might be done,
but more appropriate in the time between
the easing of harsh winter and the thought
of the approach of spring. The tree surgeons,
with chippers, trucks, and tools, their skill
from years of pruning, come to cut back
the excess and exuberance of growth,
the rot of limbs that need removal,
dead wood, thick trunks, branches
with the girth of logs, the tangled clutter
of dry, brittle twigs, all that has died
and grown too far, accumulated
and fallen away. It makes sense
of the trees for a new year of growth.
Until the pruners come and start their work,
you won't have realized how much
there was to sort out, cut, and take away.

April Snow in Kansas

Games of a quirky jet stream, or just
a lost Canadian air mass, a blast
of colder wind, and rain that should
have been comes down untimely snow,
improbable and slow, thick flakes
almost a sly cold joke mimicking
the broad white petals of magnolias
that have already shed. Snow lights
on new greening grass and tender
shoots of perennials poking up
and about to flower, this cold a pause,
perhaps a retreat, if only for a day
or two. I think about the good and bad
fortunes of time, the march of seasons,
or being stuck on a mountain
highway, outside of Santa Fe, when
a sudden snow storm snarled traffic
and I thought it best to turn and head
back south. But here it will only last
a day, then back to the rhythms
of real spring, one more season marks
your life, subtracted from the whole.

Ivy

Discouraged by chopping and chemicals
from climbing up the almost corporeal
surfaces of brick and grotesque rough stone,
the ivy persists, refuses to give up.

So now the subtle tendrils creep low
against the ground, into basement
window wells, and as if guided by a sly
insidious intelligence, they find unseen

impossible openings and infiltrate through
windows into cellar rooms where dust,
the spider webs and laziness of long-
unacknowledged guilt have stashed

in moldering, incriminating boxes all
the letters and papers that I lack
the courage to confront even as
the ivy relentlessly grows close.

The Dragonflies

Early autumn, still warm
but the plants resign to the rule
of slow drying, soon the chill
edge of seasons, and suddenly
from the thicket of tangled
shriveled fronds of the peonies
and the dense chaos of weeds
a flight of dragonflies comes out.
Back as children we called them
darning needles, and now,
both sinister and beautiful,
we see them as sly magic predators,
eating mosquitoes and other creatures
we humans might not want.
Among the fastest insects
in their swift determined flight,
their sudden presence is a pleasant
shock, their goal all but a mystery.

Travel

TRAVEL

I think of fall as time for taking in,
an audit of those things we'd hope to keep.
We come round on another year, the deep
disquiet of a bond that might have been.

But winter is again our pressing task,
to face another turning of the page
on which I write the gentle tolls of age,
and in this slowing light I only ask

for yet more journeys, first through Spanish hills,
then threading round Italian towns, with you
beside me, giving me new sight, as through
this shared geography, your pleasure fills

me with a sense of time and space well spent,
and love against the call that won't relent.

War Stories

Absurd old photographs, rediscovered
in tattered envelopes, edges curling up,
some black and white, others in color,
all fading, but even the black and white

reveal, remind me how the harsh brown dust
of that year in Vietnam invaded all.
I recognize most of the men, posed in
moments briefly freed from noise and fear.

Private Davidson in one shot, with his
jungle hat, but his thin torso shirtless,
narrow-shouldered, hairless as a teenage
boy. But that is who and what they were.

Aware and unaware of duty, place,
exiled in time, brutalities of heat
and random violence. One older man
was tasked to be there and take care of them.

Now memory gives way to hidden wounds.
And photographs – do they too suffer from
the slow toll of their own mortality,
to dust of stories we can never tell?

Ghost Town

Near empty highways, heading west,
the landscapes desolate, the dust
of half-abandoned settlements
crouched mournful by the road,

rusting broken farm machinery,
and illusions from a gas station
one hopes in service but long closed.
I drive onward into dusk,

past a broken barn, vacant houses
tumbling into time, not yet fully void
but still home to ghosts of lives that were

or could have been, wretched dwellings
too much like a body, memories, and
our own frail efforts to hold on.

CLEARING STATION

Toward the end of my time in country,
as a medic who knew how to read and write,
keep records, do reports, I was
A & D clerk for the 15th Medical Battalion's
clearing station. As such it was my job
to unzip the grim black body bags, search
through the chaos of bodies killed this way
for dog-tags, other identification, the simple
horror of what is left. Sometimes the earth
and filth of jungle itself had been scooped
into the sack. After fourteen months,
on February seventeenth, nineteen seventy-one,
I returned home, largely undamaged,
fortunate, already too old.

A Note on *La Bohème*

Something other than the haunting lines
of music, pathos grim fatality of loss,
this opera runs like an essential thread
through my life, tangled in identity,
persistent mystery. Still a child but near
the cusp of adolescent turmoil, fear,
I saw an amateur production, tacky props,
a flimsy cardboard fireplace, and yet
a famous oboist, out of retirement,
unknown to me, not only brought to life
the notes of Puccini's plangent score,
but also captured imagination and desire,
from which I'd never then be free.
Later there were spectacular renditions
where I would watch and listen
always on the edge of tears, until
the twentieth of July, twenty twelve,
and I am with a young woman friend
in Lisbon, outdoors, the Largo do Intendente.
They sang the tragic tale in Portuguese.
As always I was moved, as if the first time.
The next day I'd learn that my mother died
that very night, an ocean and a continent away.

Sleep Debt

I cannot make it balance out, the stretch
of time when I should sleep straight through
against my waking hours when all
is purposeful and clear.
At best my sleep is fitful, torn by disruptive dreams,
compounded by long travels and jet lag,
waking in some unfamiliar bed, always alone,
disoriented and forgetting where
and why I'm there, having fought for sleep
against a throbbing surge of foreign noise,
or else enclosed in total, eerie hotel hush.
The dreams unmake my waking world, distort,
dismember, recombine daytime events,
night-time fears. But stumbling with the weight
of all these years, I've lost my certainty
of which is more authentic me, and if
I've failed to pay the proper debts of sleep
before the last one comes to sum accounts.

El Campo del Príncipe, Granada

On the downhill side of this park
small restaurants and bars spread out their tables
on terraces open to the air.
I sit at late lunch, observe the Spanish hour,
and let time play out as slowly as it can,
untroubled by a heat really not so harsh,
while tiny nozzles in the frame above dispense
their gentle bursts of water misting down.
A furtive street cat, scrawny but almost
Egyptian in her face and long-eared cast,
threads her attentive way through tables, chairs.
She doesn't deign to beg, but waits, wise
from experience, for scraps of chicken,
bits of fried fish, that we drop her way,
to later disappear into the bushes of the park,
a patient survivor, indifferent to the wonders
of the Alhambra's fragile enchantments
high atop the hill above, almost
invisible and somehow not quite real.

Packing

Somehow it all must be contained, to fit
into this one black canvas duffle bag,
to heft by shoulder strap, each year more hard
on my progressively less able back.

Bare minimum of necessary clothes,
plus all the other things I think I'll need,
my vexing gadgets, cell phones, camera,
wires, converter to recharge their batteries,

and for my own run-down machine, the pills
I'm told to take, to keep a body alive and well,
a kind of balance never quite attained,
and travels, a sad thrust against the toll of time.

What are the things I will forget to pack?
A journey, one less before the trip without return.

Cat Science, Part IV: Pulga and Me

I've grown to know the people
of this place, Lisbon, almost asleep
in a dream of its vast, lost empire,
the ghosts of Portugal.
I'll move on in a day or two,
back to Spain. But for a moment
here the jet-black green-eyed cat
lying on the orange table cloth
before me knows the edgy vanity
of men, mine, caught up
in our foolish arcs of time,
wishing we could learn
just what the black cat knows.

Photograph

Later, a rediscovered photograph
perplexes and torments. A soldier stands
on a balcony, right arm gesturing up,
jungle fatigue trousers, no shirt, dog-tags
on a chain round his neck all but lost
in the coarse black forest of his chest,
illusion of virility in one whose destiny
as a man would never quite come full.
Now one can read in this picture
the confused ambivalence.

Forty years beyond the interplay
of violence and boredom that was
Vietnam, at twenty-five both too old,
yet too young, innocent, to be
fully formed, mere survival
his pressing task. Impossible to know
that he'd be little more than a lost,
bewildered traveler, weary, searching
numbing mists, waiting out
silences, telling random stories, lies.

Reliquary

I wander through old monasteries, stone
columned cloisters, museums that now display
the treasures of another age, the way
those faithful once revered a piece of bone,

a splinter thought to be part of the cross,
an object that would link one to a time
when passion and belief held strong, a prime
example of what was before faith's loss.

I stop in travels through Spain, in León
and take a rest from weariness of mind,
apart from those no longer loved, to find
serenity, a need to be alone.

Medieval relics, silent, point the way
I too will join them on that ordained day.

The River Tormes

July and the calm expanse glides past
gold and glowing monumental stones,
Salamanca, city of churches, convents,
a university, starting point of such comic,
bitter stories, literature, and no doubt
more than one hard haunting memory.

Upstream from the Roman bridge
it widens and lies placid as a mirror
beneath the depths of night, while on
the other bank I study the cathedral
and its inverted double, itself
a legendary pair, two churches
lying side by side, linked like lovers
through centuries impossible to read.

I've wandered through this place,
many times before, its storied streets.
I think that this is where so much began,
or began to end, perhaps a gentle touch,
not quite an embrace, in an almost silent
November morning, a Salamanca room.

Frómista

Little more than a small open space,
barely a town, tranquil and sun-washed,
luminous, the buildings spare and spaced
apart in the solidity of Medieval limestone,
the rounded vaults and monumental weight
of Romanesque simplicity.

I have a sense of epochs, the sift of time,
an urge to hold on against oblivion,
or just the lapse and light distortions
of a mere quarter century.

I try to read the crudely carved figures
of the capitals that crown the columns,
Biblical stories abbreviated in stone.
I meditate on the wonder of sacred emptiness
and try to recall that other time when I traveled
not alone. On a whim I've stopped in Frómista.
I get back in the car and drive on, east and south
across the Spanish plain, geography of sad recall.

Santo Domingo de Silos

The tempo of dusk fading into deeper night
at the pace of summer in Spain is so gradual
that I will linger on the near-empty terraza
of a hotel on the edge of Santo Domingo de Silos,
nurse a brandy, gaze at the hills, seeing nothing
or perhaps all there is in this moment
of one brief day, after attending vespers,
Gregorian chant of the monks, the austere
church of San Sebastián, but thinking, too,
how startled and perplexed I was, to return
after twenty-five years and find that nothing
quite conformed to memory, the shape
and texture of the place. Lisa had insisted
we come here. We shared the journey
and the rooms of night in the calm
after all desire had long been lost.
I take this evening silent and alone.

Alcalá de Henares

On this last evening in Spain
I've come to Alcalá again, a pause.
At first I notice just a few,
fantastic bricolage, ungainly huge
stick creations, the stork nests.
Then I see them everywhere;
they populate the highest roofs,
church towers, projections, parapets,
the buildings of Alcalá de Henares.
The cathedral tower holds a colony.
I stop and watch in wonder as
the storks swoop high above,
broad-winged and graceful,
silent in their circling arcs,
sentinels above the city who
define this place and yet remain
indifferent to the busy world below
where I find myself on one last day
before I end another visit,
yielding to the reality of return.

Poitiers, 11 July 2011

The gentle yet pathetic curse of calendars.
One gets caught up in anniversaries,
even though I know one day is no more
important than the next or the one before,
time all but meaningless, stretching out
in both directions. And yet on this
second Monday in July, the first day
of a conference, I find myself in Poitiers,
reading a paper, a trivial brief lecture
in my always limping Spanish, lost
in a city still filtering medieval dust,
churches yielding thick Romanesque
almost to Gothic. I want to escape,
reject the pull and recall of time,
just to give a lecture, try not to think
too much about this date, on which
my father died sixteen years ago.

Picking up the Pieces

I was an Army medic in Vietnam, December '69
to February '71. It wasn't like the movies, rather
alternating times of mind-numb tedium, then bursts
of sudden terror, routine illness, grim discoveries,
my duty to identify a mangled corpse.

But mostly I was tasked to comfort and support,
to reassure, pick up the pieces of insecurity
and the hurt of men too young to be thrown
into this swamp of violence and perplexity.

Forty years later, another kind of medic, I seem
to be the one to whom they come with aches
and insecurities, other kinds of injury.

Unaware of the depths of their own damages,
they lay out their chaos for me to sort out,
pick up the pieces, bind a nagging wound.
The medic's wound is never seen.

Salamanca

Dusk falls, the chill of the high Castilian plain
envelopes us as we walk downhill,
past magical Medieval buildings,
their monumental stone glowing warm,
almost gold, almost flesh of legend,
as we approach the Río Tormes,
the Roman bridge, the concrete places
of a book that forged a special bond.
And somehow, with you beside me
on this ancient span, sharing your vision,
passionate curiosity, I see it all
as if, despite my weary decades,
I'd never been here before or seen
these storied stones that shaped,
almost unrealized, my very life.

PUEBLA

Decades past in Mexico, I forget
the night, but it happened, not suddenly.
You were house-sitting for a woman
friend in Puebla, the place to ourselves,
and I cooked dinner. We made love
through the night until exhaustion, dawn.
For a while we tried to hold the bond.
But our lives diverged. A boy was born,
becoming a shared mystery. Later tests
denied my paternity, but I did not believe,
nor did it matter. Only with the rasp of time
did I learn there would be no other
chance at fatherhood or shared life,
and your embrace would be my last.
But I would go on wandering through
those memories, searching for you
or for another truth, my unfixed self,
lost between this endless isolation
or possible return, that touch and trust.

INDEXING

It's something that one has to do
after a book is fully written through,
to make the index, a compilation
and a kind of secret map.

I have to read through everything again,
each page, a sifting and a search.
It forces me to revisit, perhaps rethink
ideas and assertions that now surprise,

somewhat disturb, as time has gnawed away.
Not unlike the woven but now tangled text
we call a life. I hunt and scratch,
a squirrel of words. I try to find

or fabricate an order that might serve,
a sign or indicator, listing all,
but not enough and only for a while.

New Student

We think we teach the subject on the books,
while we grow old with repetitions, tired
in ways we fail to see, almost expired.
Then eagerly there comes the one who looks

for what he does not fully know he needs.
Nor does the teacher realize at first
the goal both of them seek, the secret thirst,
a dialogue between the two that feeds

the hunger of a youth who's run so far,
aching, alone in solitary search,
to find the real beneath what merely seems.

A teacher forgets who his students are,
until, lost in a fog, trying to reach
an end, the runner comes and joins his dreams.

A Coin

A curiosity, just a simple coin from 1983,
a Kennedy half-dollar. The student got it
as part of some change and considered
his find notable. I thought about the decades
in between and how much has gone by,
changed in my own life. The decade of
the eighties was mine in certain ways.
After class the student, knowing I'd had
a birthday, came up and gave me the coin
as a present. His glow of warmth
and innocence enveloped me. Then
he took me in an embrace, pressed
his slender body tight to mine. Inspired
by mere coincidence, an old coin, he
charmed me with his gift,
more than this rare half-dollar.

Body of Stories

Enjoined by some mysterious power you came
as if on mission to assuage a need
I didn't know I had, an ache for quiet
pleasure. A lean athletic grace and wit
like some dark mythic trickster god won me.
Your kind yet piercing hazel gaze
opened me to read my secrets like a book.
More than a shared and simple warmth we told
our true and necessary tales, and despite
our gap of ages, they dovetailed, fit
together, very like our storied bodies
held close and wordless in embrace.

Sly Artist

Both innocent and subtly crafty,
a warm dark glow, thin wiry form
only slowly broke through to catch
my distracted, tired attention, led
me out. Your careful reading
of a frayed body's half-forgotten
history woke old stories up.
But yours also, young and graceful,
held its stories. You are your own
beguiling work of art and one
I finally realized as you took
me in your arms and there
the power of art prevailed.

Renewal

Multiply they come, the envelopes,
reminders, notices for me to renew
a subscription, and I always hesitate,
question. Don't I already have too many
journals, magazines, news letters?
And yet the slim notice says
"one year," or "two years," more.
I think: how many more years
can or should there be? Perhaps
it's what I need. And you, eager,
lively and curious young student,
mark another offer of renewal,
this time unique, quite unexpected,
and for all that, more valuable.

Dramatis Personae

So many times we fail to realize,
until the final scene goes black
and house lights slowly come back on,
the role we were assigned to act.

I still don't know how well I played the part.
Surely I stumbled, muffed my lines.
Could I have known the man I had to seem
to a public, silent, all but invisible in the dark?

Later one came up to me, off stage, as if
to congratulate me on a performance
I did not know I gave, and it was you.
It left me startled at your warmth and praise,

to find you'd seen through costume, make up, lights,
that naked truth, a message for your need.

Cosmos

Our stories and our searches begin with the vast
riddle of infinity, the sky, how on a cloudless night
it opens up, encloses and beckons to the immensity
of space, the chill, elusive messages of stars
uncountable, almost unreal, as if another realm.

Fixed firmly on our spot of earth, we too
are lost in thought, spinning through
a cosmos that we'll never fully understand.
And yet we sleuth the endless labyrinths
of science, try to measure, comprehend.

Somehow we feel slightly alien, both within
and yet distant from the endless vibrations
of the universe, wondering: do I briefly live
in the world, or does the world live endlessly
in me? Time and matter, one coherent whole.

About the Author

WILLIAM H. CLAMURRO is Professor of Spanish at Emporia State University. He is the author of three books, *Cervantes's Novelas ejemplares: Reading Their Lessons from His Time to Ours* (2015), B*eneath the Fiction: The Contrary Worlds of Cervantes's Novelas Ejemplares* (1997), and *Language and Ideology in the Prose of Quevedo* (1991). His edition of the last four of *Cervantes's Novelas ejemplares* was published in 2011.

In addition, Prof. Clamurro is active as a musician and has performed with orchestras in Massachusetts, New Jersey, and Ohio. In Emporia, he has performed with the ESU chamber orchestra, the Emporia Symphony Orchestra, and the Mid-America Woodwind Quintet. As an undergraduate at Amherst College (class of '67), Clamurro studied creative writing with Archibald McLeish, and his poetry has been published in the *Flint Hills Review* and in other literary magazines.

www.ingramcontent.com/pod-product-compliance
Lightning Source LLC
Chambersburg PA
CBHW030944090426
42737CB00007B/531